MIRROR LAKE, WAXEN SWAN

Victoria Barragan

Newton-le-Willows

Published in the United Kingdom in 2020
by The Knives Forks And Spoons Press,
51 Pipit Avenue,
Newton-le-Willows,
Merseyside,
WA12 9RG.

ISBN 978-1-912211-64-7

Supported using public funding by
ARTS COUNCIL
ENGLAND

MIRROR LAKE, WAXEN SWAN

the cawing moon
shone clear light

whirr sparingly
silken songster heart

raiment swindlers
loom strange thread

deadly headed
black crows slept

sloe-bush bore sour fruit
for the tame sweetheart

widowed crow
hand beckoned

sprang lissom
from a raven's stronghold

seized sugar wings
like leaves of glass
tethered tight

tree stumps of
coal-black

soft split
smoke-laden bark

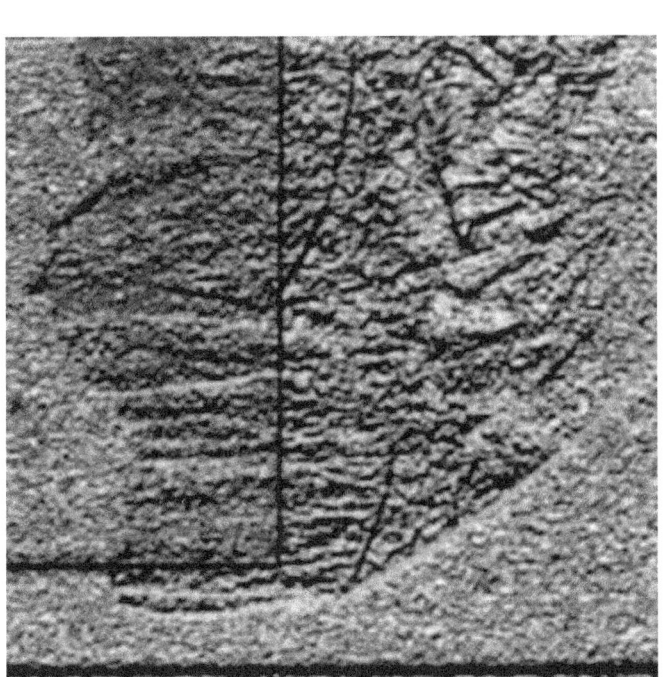

mild silence
    of a soft moss pillow

glow worms shower
    from lofty places

days passed
missing, forgotten

wits wasting like

basking blossom

ringed by honey fungus
in a glaucous slumber

canker-baked

apple tree bark

oozes amber sap

a tiny wetted hand

rubs, cups

ripens wild apples

tree branch
under fruit weight

sunbeam fence
of solitude

late summers
melted swarms

seasons dawdled
tired, sore

willow leaves
dripped yellow

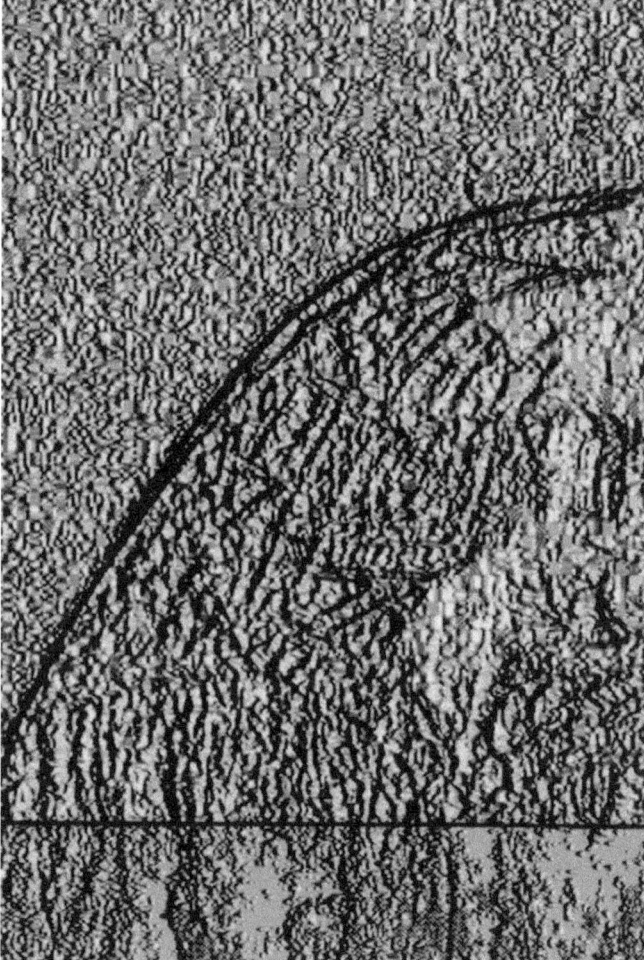

an eel's head
spurs of soft mud

water-blue smoke
rises from the marsh

moments die

in vast space

black clouds, white crested

silver motes
circling

unending lake
blue-black mirror

pebbles of polished water
seaweed smooth

heritage of grief
three hundred years deep

shame sagged
inched behind life

bitter winter's brittle palace

a thousand jagged screes

mourning shoes
of red morocco

dreaming dirge of the women

singing sword

rich death

in exchange for a song

breeze rustles
evergreens

scent illusion
tobacco strong

sleep memory
of a falling place

this thought
insect delicate

shock twin

unimpressed double

a lover crept by, asleep

he is dead and gone, she told the swallows

fire blighted
blossom pyre

crumbling leaf

the end, he remembered

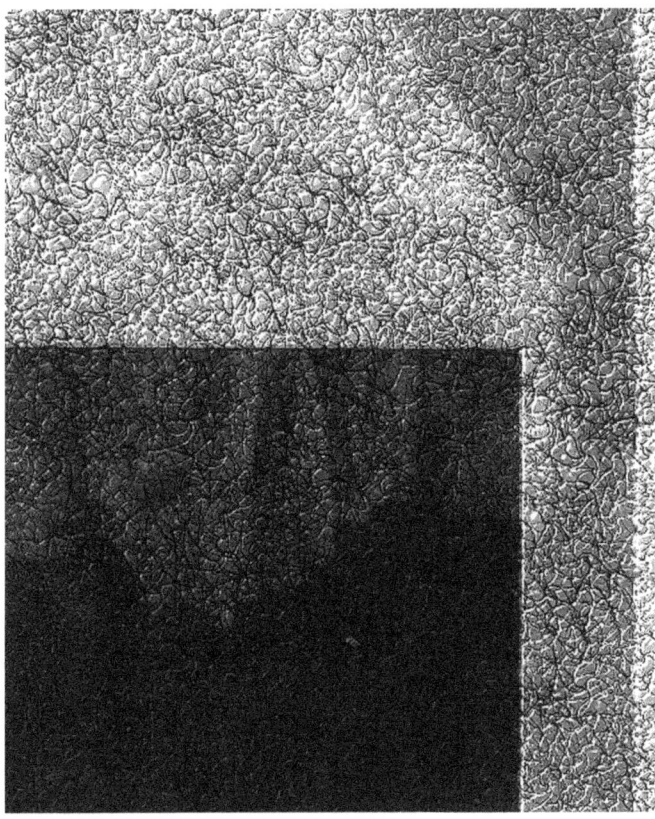

flooded gutters
culvert dark

sharp stones stream with water

roots flow free of earth

the drowned

throw waves ashore

in the wake
promise flocked

www.ingramcontent.com/pod-product-compliance
Lightning Source LLC
Chambersburg PA
CBHW032102040426
42449CB00007B/1155